MW00395413

What should I use?

The technology of simple machines

David Drew

Illustrated by Ester Kasepuu and Roman Stolz

CONTENTS

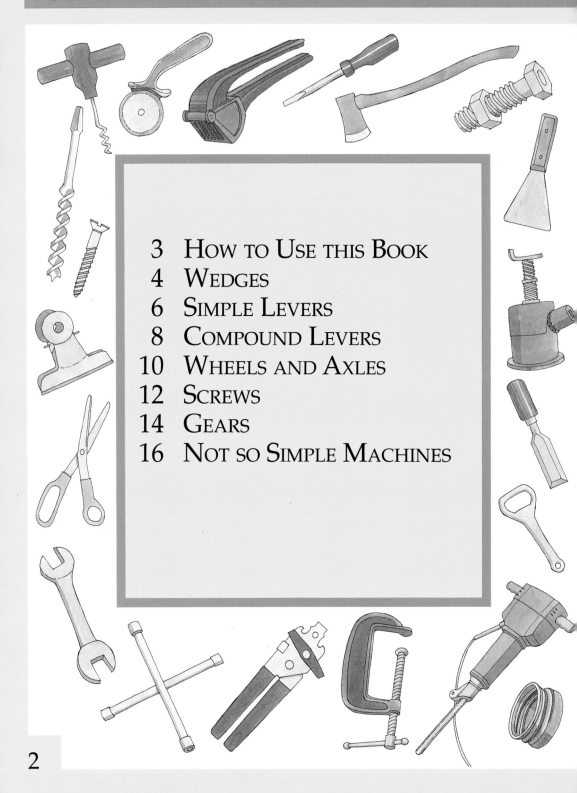

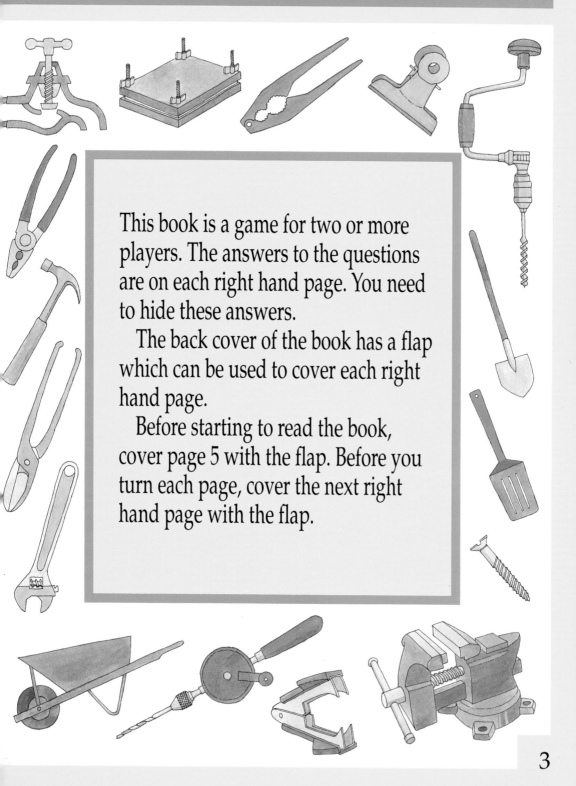

This book is a game for two or more players. The answers to the questions are on each right hand page. You need to hide these answers.

The back cover of the book has a flap which can be used to cover each right hand page.

Before starting to read the book, cover page 5 with the flap. Before you turn each page, cover the next right hand page with the flap.

What should I use? Should I use:

1

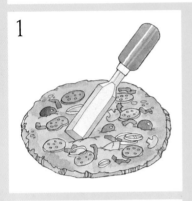

the chisel
to cut the pizza?

2

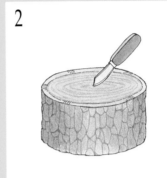

the penknife
to split the firewood?

3

the spatula
to break the concrete

What would you choose?

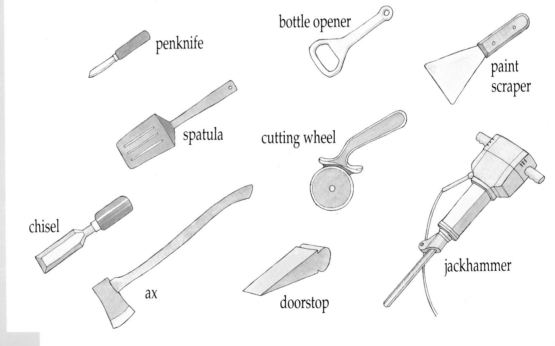

penknife

bottle opener

paint
scraper

spatula

cutting wheel

chisel

ax

doorstop

jackhammer

I'd choose to use:

1

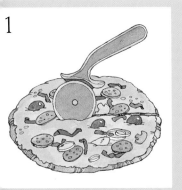

the cutting wheel to cut the pizza.

2

the ax to split the firewood.

3

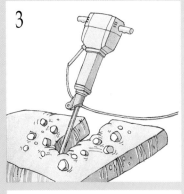

the jackhammer to break the concrete.

All three of these machines are wedges.

Wedges work like this:

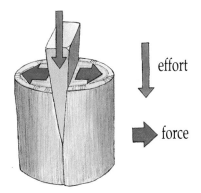

effort

force

A wedge is an example of an inclined plane.

A wedge produces a powerful force at right angles to the direction in which it is moving (the effort).

One of these machines is *not* a wedge. Can you find it?

The bottle opener is not a wedge: it's a simple lever.

What should I use? Should I use:

1

the shovel
to open the lid?

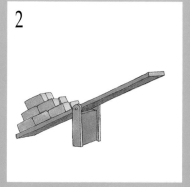

2

the seesaw
to carry the bricks?

3

the pitchfork
to catch the fish?

What would you choose?

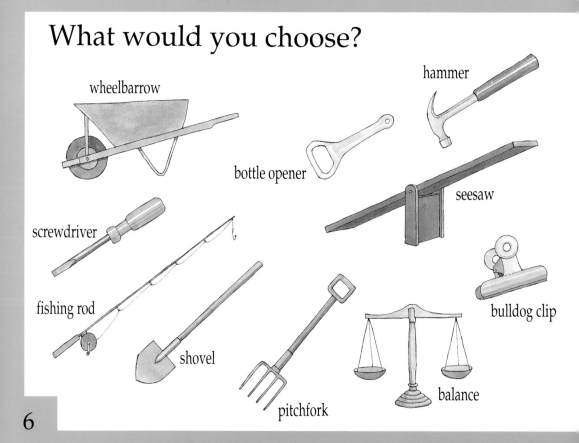

wheelbarrow

hammer

bottle opener

screwdriver

seesaw

fishing rod

bulldog clip

shovel

pitchfork

balance

I'd choose to use:

1

the screwdriver
to open the lid.

2

the wheelbarrow
to carry the bricks.

3

the fishing rod
to catch the fish.

All three of these machines are simple levers.

Simple levers work like this:

When you apply effort to a lever, the lever turns around a point called the fulcrum, in order to move a load.

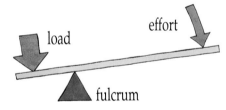

load

effort

fulcrum

First class lever

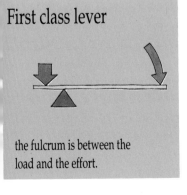

the fulcrum is between the load and the effort.

Second class lever

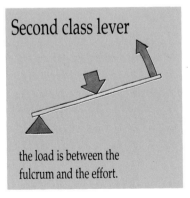

the load is between the fulcrum and the effort.

Third class lever

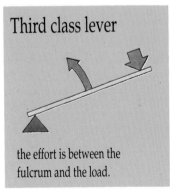

the effort is between the fulcrum and the load.

One of these machines is *not* a simple lever. Can you find it?

The bulldog clip is not a simple lever: it's a compound lever.

What should I use? Should I use:

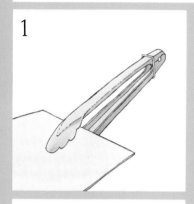

1

the tongs
to cut the cardboard?

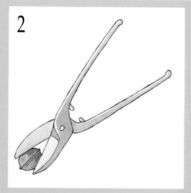

2

the tinsnips
to crack the walnut?

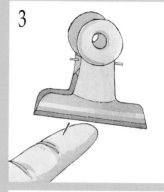

3

the bulldog clip to
remove the splinter?

What would you choose?

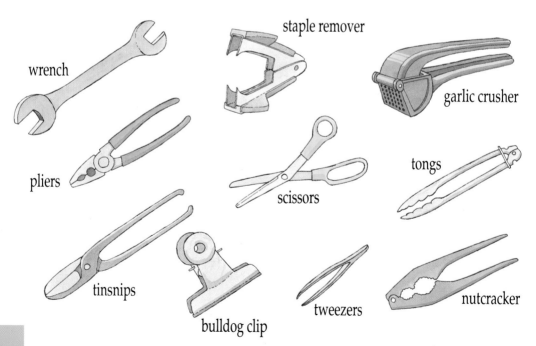

wrench

staple remover

garlic crusher

pliers

scissors

tongs

tinsnips

bulldog clip

tweezers

nutcracker

I'd choose to use:

1

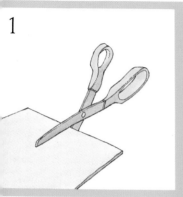

the scissors
to cut the cardboard.

2

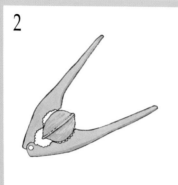

the nutcracker
to crack the walnut.

3

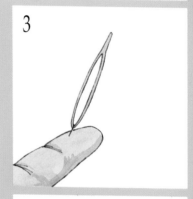

the tweezers to
remove the splinter.

All three of these machines are compound levers.

Compound levers work like simple levers:

The only difference is that compound levers are two simple levers that move around the same fulcrum.

First class lever

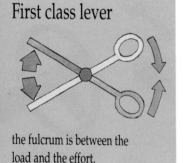

the fulcrum is between the load and the effort.

Second class lever

the load is between the fulcrum and the effort.

Third class lever

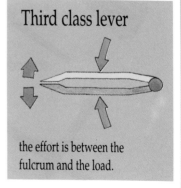

the effort is between the fulcrum and the load.

One of these machines is *not* a compound lever. Can you find it?

The wrench is not a compound lever: it's a wheel and axle.

What should I use? Should I use:

1

the eggbeater
to loosen the wheel?

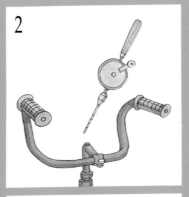

2

the drill to tighten
the handlebars?

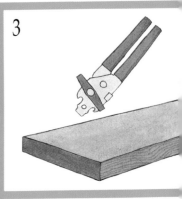

3

the can opener
to drill a hole?

What would you choose?

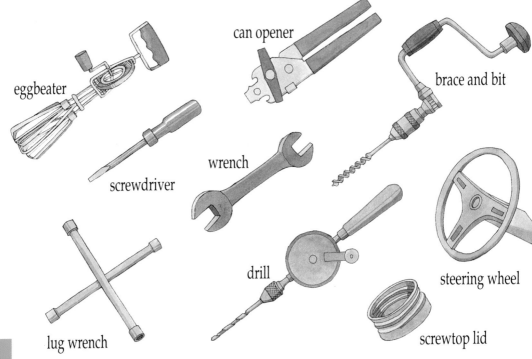

can opener

eggbeater

brace and bit

screwdriver

wrench

steering wheel

drill

lug wrench

screwtop lid

I'd choose to use:

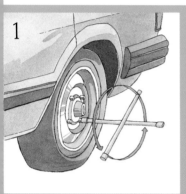

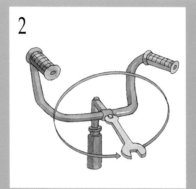

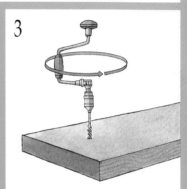

1	2	3
the lug wrench to loosen the wheel.	the wrench to tighten the handlebars.	the brace and bit to drill a hole.

All three of these machines are wheels and axles.

A wheel and axle works like this:

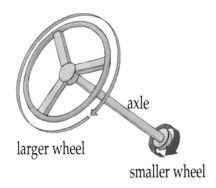

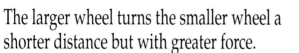

axle

larger wheel

smaller wheel

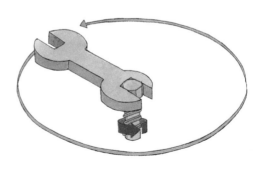

The larger wheel turns the smaller wheel a shorter distance but with greater force.

A wrench turns a bolt in the same way as a large wheel turns an axle.

One of these machines is *not* a wheel and axle. Can you find it?

What should I use? Should I use:

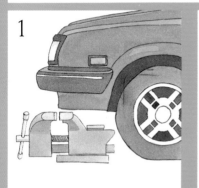

1

the vise
to raise the car?

2

the C clamp
to open the bottle?

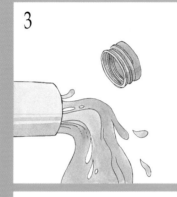

3

the screwtop lid
to stop the water?

What would you choose?

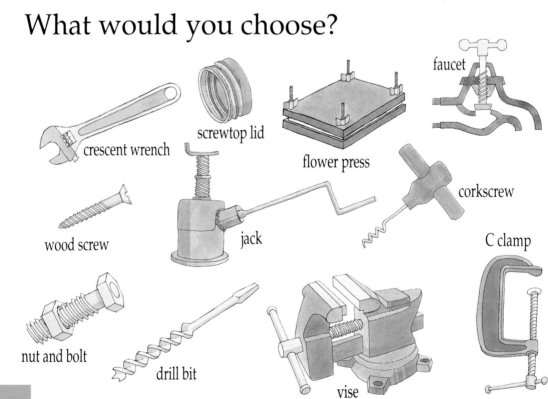

crescent wrench

screwtop lid

flower press

faucet

corkscrew

wood screw

jack

C clamp

nut and bolt

drill bit

vise

I'd choose to use:

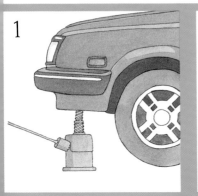

1

the jack
to raise the car.

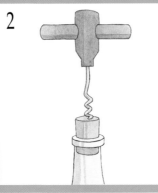

2

the corkscrew
to open the bottle.

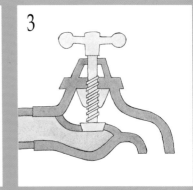

3

the faucet
to stop the water.

All three of these machines are screws.

Screws work like this:

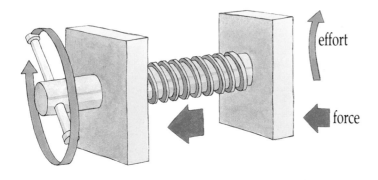

effort

force

A screw produces a powerful force at right
angles to the direction in which the screw
is rotated (the effort).

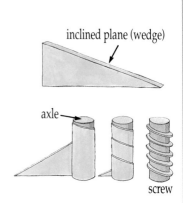

inclined plane (wedge)

axle

screw

A screw is an example of
an inclined plane. It is a wedge
wrapped around an axle.

One of these machines is *not* a screw. Can you find it?

What should I use? Should I use:

 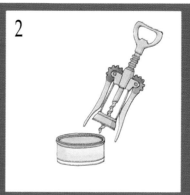 

1	2	3
the alarm clock to beat the eggs?	the corkscrew to open the can?	the crescent wrench to wake me up?

What would you choose?

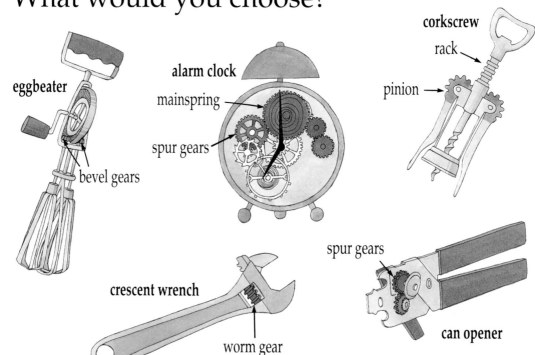

eggbeater

bevel gears

alarm clock

mainspring

spur gears

corkscrew

rack

pinion

crescent wrench

worm gear

spur gears

can opener

I'd choose to use:

1

the eggbeater
to beat the eggs.

2

the can opener
to open the can.

3

the alarm clock
to wake me up.

All three of these machines make use of gears.

Gears transfer movement from one part of a machine to another.

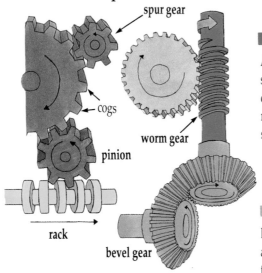

spur gear

cogs

worm gear

pinion

rack

bevel gear

■ spur gears
Spur gears are two gear wheels which intermesh: one wheel drives the other at the same speed but in the opposite direction.

■ worm gear
A worm gear is a shaft with a screw thread: it changes the direction of the machine's movement and slows down its speed.

■ rack and ■ pinion
Rack and pinion gears combine to convert circular movement to back-and-forth movement.

■ bevel gears
Bevel gears intermesh at an angle to change the direction of the movement in a machine.

One of these machines includes a wedge, a simple lever, a compound lever, a wheel and axle, and a set of gears, all in one. Can you find it?

1 compound first class lever

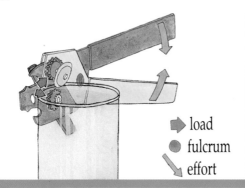

load
fulcrum
effort

2 wheel and axle

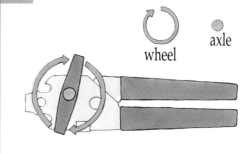

wheel
axle

3 wedge

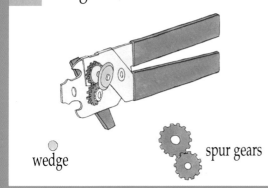

wedge
spur gears

4 simple second class lever

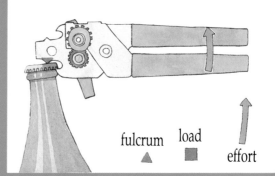

fulcrum   load
effort

How many machines can you find:

in one eggbeater?

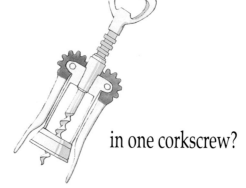

in one corkscrew?